Brandy Miller

Creating A Character Backstory

By Brandy Miller

Creating A Character Backstory

Copyright 2013 by Brandy Miller. All rights reserved.

Published by TokaySEO, Euless, Texas.

No part of this publication may be reproduced, stored in a retrieval system, or transmitted in any form or by any means, electronic, mechanical, photocopying, recording, scanning, or otherwise, except as permitted under section 107 or 108 of the 1976 United States Copyright Act, without the prior written permission of the publisher.

Limit of Liability/Disclaimer of Warranty: While the publisher and author have used their best efforts in preparing this book, they make no representations or warranties with respect to the accuracy or completeness of the contents of this book and specifically disclaim any implied warranties of merchantability or fitness for a particular purpose. No warranty may be created or extended by sales representatives or written sales materials. The advice and strategies contained herein may not be suitable for your situation. Neither the publisher nor the author shall be liable for any loss of profit or other commercial damages, including, but not limited to, special, incidental, consequential, or other damages.

TokaySEO's books are available at special quantity discounts to use as premiums and sales promotions, or for use in corporate training programs. To place a bulk order, please contact the TokaySEO at info@tokayseo.com.

ISBN-13: 978-1482652048

ISBN-10: 1482652048
Printed in the United States of America

Brandy Miller

Table Of Contents

Chapter 1: What is My Purpose. 10

Chapter 2: What's My Problem. 14

Chapter 3: Who Am I. 19

Chapter 4: My Faith Life. 23

Chapter 5: A Day In My Life. 26

Chapter 6: My Greatest Fears. 29

Chapter 7: My Greatest Dreams. 32

Chapter 8: My Talents. 35

Chapter 9: My Skills. 38

Chapter 10: The Best (and Worst) About Me 42

Chapter 11: The Secrets I Keep 46

Chapter 12: What Don't I Know. 50

Chapter 13: The Worst Day Of My Life. 53

Chapter 14: The Best Day Of My Life. 56

Chapter 15: My First Love and My Current Love Interest 58

Chapter 16: My Best Friend. 62

Chapter 17: My Worst Enemy. 65

Creating A Character Backstory

Chapter 18: Meet My Family............................. 68

Chapter 19: My Mother, My Father, And I.................. 71

Chapter 20: Life At Home............................... 74

Dedication

"Dedicated with great love to the many role players in my life who taught me all that I know about the importance of a character backstory especially my husband, Randy, my son, Eddie, my foster son, Edward, my brother, Kevin, and my friends David Goodner, Christopher Jackson, and Stephen Johnson with whom I spent many pleasant hours. Also dedicated to my publisher, Casey Watkins, without whose tireless efforts on my behalf this book would not have come to be."

Creating A Character Backstory

Preface
A shortcut to believable characters

The hardest task most authors have is creating believable characters with a consistent voice. Taking the time to create a character backstory allows you, as the author, to get to know your character inside and out. You'll learn about their relationships, their strengths and weaknesses, even their talents and skills. By the time you are done creating this character, it won't be hard to understand why they do what they do or to think like them when they are placed in a challenging situation. Furthermore, you'll have a written reference so you don't have to keep all these details in your head. This will reduce the time it takes to edit your story later by preventing careless errors, like having your character participating in an event that takes place before the character was even born!

More is always better

The exercises in this book are designed to help you create a rich, full backstory for your character. You may think you are not going to use these details and be tempted to skip an exercise. However, I urge you to go ahead and do the exercises anyway. More information is always better than less. You may think you won't need to know who your character's great grandmother is, when she was born, or when she got married – but knowing this information can provide you with inspiration on names (perhaps your character's first or middle name is inherited from a great-grandparent), treasured items that a character owns (the afghan on her bed is inherited from her great-grandma Jenna, who died 7 years before she was born), and suggest items that might be found in a setting that a character visits.

Helping overcome writer's block

One of the best things about taking the time to create rich, deep characters is that their backstory can provide inspiration for overcoming writer's block. When you're stuck and don't know what else to write, review the backstory you created for them. Introduce someone from their past, force them to tackle a long held fear, or challenge them to overcome a weakness. This can help you either find new problems and challenges for your character to overcome, driving the plot forward a few paces, or can provide new insights that help the character find a previously overlooked solution, or offer connections that were not possible for the character to make with their given knowledge.

Work sheets for this ebook

I have made a couple of worksheets for this book. You can find them here

http://40daywriter.com/tools/character-sheets/

| Creating A Character Backstory

What is My Purpose?

Every character has a purpose

Every character you create for your story has a role to play. From the hero to the villain and everyone in between, these characters will provide support or act as obstacles to the success of the hero. There are eight primary purposes that a character can fulfill: the hero, the herald, the mentor, the sidekick, the shape shifter, the gate keeper, the minion, and the villain. We'll examine the role each of these purposes play in the story and why they matter.

The hero

A story without a hero is like a joke without a punch line – boring and pointless. The hero allows the reader to focus his or her attention and identify with the action in the story. The hero doesn't always have to be a willing hero, some of the more interesting characters in stories do not start out wanting to be a hero. However, the character must have sufficient moral reserves that when they see the nature of the need, they are moved to action.

The herald

The job of the herald is to call the hero to action. The herald announces the problem and gives the hero his quest. If the hero does not at first want to accept the quest, the herald will create situations where the hero is confronted with the pain his decision to refuse is causing others. Eventually, this creates a moral dilemma for the hero which can only be resolved by deciding to accept the quest. The herald never forces the hero to do his bidding, but he can certainly make life for a reluctant herald miserable until he does. A perfect example of this is Gandalf in The Hobbit.

The mentor

Advisor and friend to the hero, the mentor is often someone older and more experienced who helps the hero discover and develop his hidden talents. When the hero confronts problems that he cannot overcome, or experiences a major setback, the mentor provides the advice or the help the character needs to get past the obstacle and make progress once more on his journey. There are many stories where the herald and the mentor are combined into a single character.

The sidekick

What would Batman be without Robin? Or Frodo without Sam? Or Harry without Ron and Hermione? The sidekick not only provides useful assistance to the hero throughout his journey, but also provides the encouragement and moral support needed to keep going when things are darkest and the temptation to quit is strongest. A sidekick might be a love interest, a best friend, or a sibling. It is someone the character knows well and can trust to be reliable and dependable. The downside of the sidekick is that sometimes they slow the hero down because they are not usually as competent. However, when the sidekick gets hurt because of something the villain does it can be a powerful motivator for the hero to move forward in finding a solution to the problem.

The shape shifter

Uncertain loyalties and questionable behavior define the shape shifter. Even though the character may be introduced as an ally, there is something in their background that prevents the others from fully trusting them. Furthermore, they exhibit behaviors that call their true motives into question and can even make them very unlikable. Snape is a perfect example of a shape shifter character type, where his motives were doubted by everyone until the moment when he was exonerated.

The gate keeper

Gate Keepers are not necessarily enemies, but present obstacles to the Hero on his path to solving the problem. As their name suggests, the gate keeper holds the key to the final solution but the hero must first either win the gate keeper to his side or defeat him altogether to get that key. The gate keeper often holds secrets the hero needs in order to succeed, or is a link to someone with the necessary skills to help the hero.

The minion

Acting as the villain's very own sidekick, the minion supports and helps the villain in accomplishing his or her goals. The minion is not necessarily a bad person. The minion may have been deceived into believing the villain is working for good, or the minion may have been pressured into helping by threats from the villain. However, the minion does and can present a serious threat to the hero and his support team. Someone who does evil believing it is good is not going to be any less deadly because he is being deceived. This person can be turned toward the side of good, but it won't be easy. A lot of it will hinge on how he has been treated by the hero and his team up until that point.

The villain

Every story needs a villain, that bad guy you love to hate. Defeating the villain allows the hero to solve the problem, restore life to a state of relative normal, and allow the hero to relax for a while before being called to solve his next big problem.

Exercise:

1. First, choose the purpose of this character and fill that in on your character sheet (http://40daywriter.com/tools/character-sheets/).
2. Then, write a short story from this character's perspective in which he meets both the hero (if he is the hero, write about meeting one of the support team – either mentor, herald, side kick, or shape shifter) as well as one of the opposition forces, such as the gate keeper, minion, or villain himself.

| Creating A Character Backstory

What's My Problem?

Problems drive plot

Every character in a good story has a problem. In fact, the plot revolves around how each character overcomes the challenges he faces while trying to solve his problem. The difference between the villain and the hero is what they are willing to do to solve their problems. The hero will usually do everything in his power to preserve life while the villain considers the goal more important than the lives of the people he knows. Is he willing to break laws? Is he willing to sacrifice friends and family? Is he willing to sacrifice himself? The bigger the problem is that he must face, the greater the test of his character.

Rules for problems

The problem you give your character to solve can be epic, but it must follow some basic rules. The first rule is that it must be believable. The second rule is that it must be appropriate to the role the character plays. The third rule is that it must be urgent. The fourth and final rule is that it must be attainable. If the problem you create doesn't follow these four rules, readers are unlikely to be interested or to stay interested in your writing.

Creating believable problems

The world you create has certain boundaries to it. There are things that are possible, and there are things that just aren't possible. If your story is set in modern day Earth, for instance, we do not yet have the ability for human beings to travel to Mars but we are close. It is conceivable that a hero could come up with that technology if the need were great enough. If your story is set in the 1600's, however, there is really no way at all that a character could put together all of the things necessary for such a trip. It would require technology that they simply didn't have at the time and knowledge that hadn't been uncovered yet. So, facing a character from the 1600's with the necessity of travelling to Mars creates an unbelievable problem and readers are unlikely to buy into the story.

An attainable problem

Attainability is an important factor in creating believable problems. If the solution to the problem is that a giant ship is created which transports all of life on Earth to another planet, the reader must believe not only that it is possible but that it is possible for the hero to do it. If the hero starts off the book with absolutely no power, no money, no contacts, and no expertise in what it will take to create such a ship and make it flight worthy, the reader is unlikely to believe that he or she is capable of solving the problem even if the hero knows what needs to be done.

At the beginning of the Harry Potter series, Harry Potter didn't have what it would take to defeat Voldemort completely. An eleven year old, untrained Harry Potter facing off against a fully manifested and completely capable Voldemort would not have been believable or exciting. The rules of that world would not have allowed Harry to survive such an encounter. He didn't have enough help, enough knowledge, or enough skill to do it. This is why, although we were introduced to the notion of Voldemort in book 1 and the ultimate task Harry would face of defeating him, it isn't until the last book when Harry had the time to develop his talents and skills and to gather a more impressive group of helpers that the final showdown takes place.

An appropriate problem

The problem faced by the hero must be worthy of the hero. While being unable to open a jar of mayonnaise or locate a misplaced envelope are problems, they aren't problems that are worthy of the time and effort of a hero because these are problems easily solved by just about anyone. It's not much of a story if the jar of mayonnaise is opened by the hero's wife on page number 2. When you establish a problem for the hero, the problem needs to be big enough that it can't be quickly or easily solved. The problem also needs to be something that the hero will require help to resolve.

If this is a problem facing the supporting characters such as the mentor, herald, or side kick the problem should in some way lead toward helping the hero solve his big problem. For the herald, the problem may be that he has to convince the hero to get involved. For the mentor, it will be some problem which requires either advanced skills or a skill set that the hero does not possess. For the side kick, the problem will be something that he or she cannot solve by themselves but which the hero can. Solving the problem of the side kick can lead to discovering something or learning something that then leads to them overcoming their main problem.

Creating a sense of urgency

Limiting the amount of time a character has to complete a task is one of the best ways to create a sense of urgency. After all, given enough time it's possible to do just about anything, but only an expert can solve a problem when given a very short of time to work. If the hero doesn't have the needed expertise, he'll have to find the person who does – which will take up even more of his limited time.

A second way to create a sense of urgency is to put lives at stake based on the outcome. If the hero fails, people will die. This creates not only a sense of urgency but speaks to the morality of our hero. If the hero didn't care about saving lives, he might not take up the problem at all.

Exercise:

Write one sentence describing the problem your character faces. For example, "Robert James must defeat the evil scientist Nikolas Von Murchenstein before he can deploy his biological weapon and destroy the world." On your character sheet, summarize that problem in two to three words and write it down in the problem area.

Then, write a short story of 400-500 words in which your character first encounters the problem. In the midst of this short story, you will need to answer these questions:

1. What is the problem?

Creating A Character Backstory

2. Why does it matter?
3. Why does it matter right now?
4. Why is your character the only person who can solve this problem?
5. What resources (skills, talents, special abilities, people he knows, things he owns or has access to) does your character have that will help him overcome this problem?
6. What resources does he lack but will need to solve it?

Brandy Miller

Who Am I?

What is my name?

Creating a memorable character begins with giving him or her a name. The name should be chosen carefully and should represent something important about that character. You expect something different from a character named Skinny Bob than you do from a character named Hugh Fitzgibbon, for instance. Skinny Bob sounds like he might belong in a group of teenagers, but Hugh Fitzgibbon sounds as if he might be at home in a mansion or high class setting. Of course, one of the best techniques to use is to place someone like Skinny Bob in an unexpected setting very early on to get the reader asking questions right away. If Skinny Bob is attending a party at a mansion, the reader has all kinds of questions about why he's there, how he got there, and so half of the work of drawing them in has already been done for you.

What is my gender?

Gender is built into our very genetic code. It begins to exert an influence on us in the womb, flooding our bodies with hormones as we grow and changing the structure and operations of our brains as well as our bodies. It is something to consider carefully. After we emerge from the womb, gender continues to play a role in our growth and development. Many of your character's responses to other people will come from their gender, influencing their point of view in subtle and not-so-subtle ways. While a fully grown man's response to stress is fight-or-flight, a fully grown woman's response to stress is to gather with other women and form a protective circle around the children.

If your character is not human, or if gender is not an element in the race of the species you are writing about, that will mean huge changes in the dynamics of interpersonal relationships. Be aware of this, and write accordingly. If your character is born one gender but decides to declare another gender, realize that this won't change the influence of their own natural hormones. Those things will still be there, working on them in the background. If they take hormone supplements to overcome their natural hormones, these are likely to have unexpected side effects because they aren't natural to the body and because they are fighting the natural hormones that already exist. Make sure that your writing acknowledges this, or you'll risk losing credibility in the eyes of the reader, or else give the reader a very good reason why this doesn't affect your particular character.

How old am I?

Age sets limits and boundaries for your character in terms of the number and kinds of life experiences they are capable of having. Teenagers cannot be grandparents. It's a physical impossibility. If you decide, as the writer, to challenge those limits you need to be prepared to explain how it is possible in a way that is believable to the reader. How you resolve your challenge determines the genre of the story you will be writing. If you decide to use cloning or time travel to make a teenager into a grandparent, you have created science fiction. If you decide that this particular teenager can be a grandparent because he's actually not a teenager at all but has had a spell placed on him that stops him from aging, then you have created fantasy.

When was I born?

The point in history where your character enters the story determines what events will be happening around him or her, the objects available for their use in resolving problems, the behavior of the people around them, the way they dress, and the habits they are likely to form. When writing about the past, make sure you do the research so that you know what your character is likely to encounter. If you decide to change something about the historical past, make sure that you have a reasonable explanation for how it is possible or you will lose credibility in the eyes of your reader.

Where was I born?

Where your character was born will impact the language he or she speaks, the laws that affect him or her, the things that are considered acceptable behavior and those that aren't. It will also affect the kinds of plants and animals the character is familiar with, and the kinds of things that are completely unknown. It will shape the viewpoint he or she holds on people from foreign lands and even different areas of the land they currently live in and all of this should be taken into consideration when creating a character.

Creating A Character Backstory

Exercise:

Step 1. On your character sheet, fill in the character's name, gender, age, birth date and place.

Step 2. Write a story of 400-500 words about the day of your character's birth, hatching, manifestation, assembly, or release from the cloning mechanism that created him or her. After all, this is fiction, so a birth doesn't necessarily have to mean literal birth. In the midst of the story, be sure to answer what the character's name is, what gender he or she is, as well as where and when in history this event takes place.

My Faith Life

Faith is what you believe about how the universe, the world, and all of the things that populate it came into being. Your faith life is how you live out that belief in your day to day activities and interactions with other people. Your character's faith and how they live that belief out will impact every decision they make, every hope they have, and how they address their fears. It will also determine what they decide to do when confronted with someone who is out to harm them, or who has done something to hurt them.

A character who believes they are the product of an accident and not that of a divine being will behave very differently from a character who truly believes that his life is a creation of an all-powerful and all-knowing divine being. Likewise, a character who believes that the god or gods who created him did so out of love and for the purpose of showing love to others will react very differently than a character who believes that the god or gods who created him did so for their own purposes with no particular care or thought given to their creation's needs.

What is my belief about how the world was created?

How does your character believe that the universe and all the things that populate it came into being? Does your character's belief match the events that really happened? Why does your character believe that the universe was created? Does he believe it serves a purpose? If so, what purpose does it serve? What evidence does he find in his world to support that belief? What things lead him to doubt his own beliefs?

How do I live out this belief?

What does your character do in his daily life that reflects his beliefs? How does it impact his relationships with other people? How does it impact the way that he treats people who do not believe the way he does? How does it impact the way that he treats those who have hurt him? How does it impact the way that he treats those who are lower in status than he is?

Do I believe it is important to share my belief with others?

Why does he want to share his beliefs with others? What does he feel other people will gain by believing as he does? What does your character believe will happen if he does not share his beliefs with others? What does he feel will happen to those who do not share his beliefs? Why does he believe it is that other people do not share his beliefs? When your character does share his beliefs, how does he do so?

Am I alone in this belief or do I share it with a group?

Is your character's belief system something he came up with on his own or does he belong to a group of like-minded individuals? Was it something he was taught by his parents or the people who raised him? If this belief is a shared belief, what are the rules for behavior his group expects of its members? What things are forbidden for members of the group to do? What things are encouraged but not expected? What are the penalties for failing to follow the rules of the group?

Does the way I live my beliefs match the expectations of the group I belong to?

If your character belongs to an organized faith system, or religion, does what he believe and the way that he lives it match with the beliefs of the group and their expectations? If not, what is different? What parts of his religion does he accept? What parts does he reject and why? What risks is he taking in setting himself apart from the group? What consequences might he face because of his differences?

Exercise:

Step 1. Fill in the faith section on your character sheet using the 5 questions addressed in this chapter.

Step 2. Create a creation mythos for your character's faith. Describe what existed prior to creation, and how each item of creation was formed, and why. If you need an example of what a creation story might look like, look up Genesis chapter 1 online or in any Bible and read it. Your creation story can be in the form of a poem, as the first chapter of Genesis is, or a short story.

| Creating A Character Backstory

A Day In My Life

Although your character only lives on paper, if your story is to be believable the character must have a life and a personality that exist outside of the story. It is up to you, as an author, to create a believable life for your character, and part of doing that is to determine what their daily routine was like before the story began. Creating this routine in advance will help you maintain consistency and help you to accurately represent how your character would handle variations in that routine.

What is the first thing I do in the morning?

The first thing we do in the morning is often a huge indicator of what our priorities are in life, and this is just as true for any character you create. For a character whose focus in life is faith based, the first thing might be to kneel down and pray. For a character whose primary focus in life is money, the first thing might be to check their stock portfolio or balance their checkbook. For a character whose primary focus in life is fun, the first thing might be to play a video game.

Where do I spend the majority of my day?

Is your character a student? Does he or she work at a job? Do they own their own business? Are they a clergy member or a government official? Are they a stay-at-home mother? Each of these roles will determine not only where they spend the majority of their day but what they do as well. A stay-at-home mom might actually spend a lot of time in a van, transporting her kids and other neighborhood kids to and from various activities.

Who do I see every day?

Where your character spends his or her day determines who they are likely to see. This is where the details matter. For example, if your character spends a lot of time at school, he or she is likely to see not only the teachers and students but also the janitors, the cafeteria lady, the school secretary, the principal, the guidance counselor, the vice principal, and possibly even some parent volunteers. Who does your character notice? Who do they ignore? A character who believes that status determines importance isn't likely to notice that janitor or cafeteria lady unless they have a particular reason to do so.

What groups do I belong to?

In every setting where people gather, there will be groups that form. How does your character fit in to the various groups? Do they belong to one? Do they move among all of the groups fluidly? Are they on the outside, for some reason, of the various groups? If so, what is keeping them from being a part of them?

What do I do to relax?

When it's time to leave that place where most of your character's time is spent, what do they do to relax? Where do they go? Who do they bring with them? The choices made about what to do to relax are things that help define your character's personality.

How do I end my day?

Does your character work until he or she collapses in exhaustion? Do they have a set routine? Knowing the answers to these questions can provide you with inspiration in how to introduce elements that interrupt that routine and cause character growth and change.

Exercise:

Step 1. Sketch out your character's daily routine using the questions in this chapter as guidelines on your character sheet.

Step 2. Write a short story of 400-500 words detailing a day in the life of your character.

My Greatest Fears

Fear may well be false evidence appearing real, but fear is a reality for every human being. Our fears define our behavior. Courage isn't the absence of fear, but the choice we make to confront the fear and deal with it. Knowing what your character fears most can help you develop plot ideas and creates a believable character that will resonate with your readers.

Who do I fear most?

Who is the one person whose very name strikes fear into the soul of your character? Why does this person cause them so much fear? What would they do to avoid this person? What have they thought about doing to get this person out of their life? How far would they be willing to go to get this person out of their life?

Who do I fear losing most?

Who is the most important person in your character's life? Why is this person so important to your character? How long have they known this person? How far would your character be willing to go to recover this person? What would he or she be willing to lose to regain this person's presence in their life? What would they do if they lost this person because of a choice they made? What would they do if they lost this person because of something someone else did? What is the one thing that would lead them to leave this person behind or to break off the relationship with them?

What do I fear losing most?

What is your character's most prized possession? Why is this item so important to your character? How long have they had the item in their possession? Does the item possess any special properties or characteristics? What does the item do? How would your character feel if they did lose the item? How far would they be willing to go to recover the item if it were stolen or lost? What would they be willing to lose to regain it? What is the one thing that would inspire them to give this thing away or to destroy it?

Where do I fear being most?

When your character envisions their worst nightmare, where are they? Is this a real place or an imagined place? What is it that makes this place so frightening to them? What experience did they have in the past that led them to fear this place? What would they be willing to do to avoid being there? How much would they be willing to sacrifice in order to avoid this place? What is the one incentive that could be offered that would inspire them to willingly go to this place?

What do I fear doing most?

On a list of things your character hopes never, ever to have to do, what is at the top of that list? What would they rather die than be forced to do? What is the only thing that could inspire them to overcome this fear? What would they be willing to do to avoid doing this? How far are they willing to go to avoid it?

Exercise

Step 1. Write down your character's fears on their character sheet

Step 2. Pick one of the fears your character has and write a short story in which they are forced to confront that fear. They do not have to overcome it. This story can take place at any point in your character's history – past, present, or future.

Creating A Character Backstory

My Greatest Dreams

Just as we are motivated by our fears, our dreams provide a different kind of motivation for us depending on how strong they are. Exploring your character's hopes will help you to better understand how to motivate your character during those moments of despair and darkness by having someone remind them of who they want to become.

What do I dream of being some day?

Children may dream of becoming a doctor, lawyer, teacher, or other professional depending upon who they view as valuable in their community. For example, a medieval peasant may aspire to become a knight because of the high status that knights of their time carry. Someone who is an adult and already has a profession may secretly desire to do something different. Perhaps they want to own their own business or even become a performing artist. Do they believe that it is truly possible? Are they willing to work for it? Do they actively seek out opportunities to help them make this dream a reality, or is it just something they think about from time to time?

How do I want people to see me some day?

Does your character dream of changing the way people view him or her? Do they feel unimportant now and hope that someday people will see them as important? Are they unknown now but hope someday to be famous? Are they poor now but hope someday to be rich? Do they feel powerless right now but someday hope to be seen as powerful? Why do they want people to see them this way? How do they think it will change their life for the better if people were to see them this way? What are they willing to do to have people see them this way? What sacrifices are they willing to make?

Where do I want to live someday?

Has your character always dreamed of living in the mountains? Does your character dream of traveling to Mars or other locations in space? Does your character want simply to own their own home? Does your character want to live in a foreign land? Why do they want to live there? What would it mean to your character to live there? What is your character willing to do to get there? What steps have they already taken to make this dream a reality? How have those efforts worked out? How will he or she handle things if they never achieve that goal? What sacrifices are they going to have to make to achieve that dream?

When I die, what do I want written about me?

When your character thinks of death, who do they want at their funeral? What do they want people to say about them? Have they thought about this often or never at all? What steps will they have to take to make this a reality? Have they already taken steps to accomplish that goal? How far are they on the road to getting what they want? How far do they think they have come?

Exercise:

Creating A Character Backstory

Step 1. Write down the dreams that your character has, using the questions in this segment as a guide.

Step 2. Write a short story in which your character either achieves a dream, or comes close to achieving that dream. How does it happen? How does your character feel? Is it everything they imagined it would be, or do they find themselves disappointed with the results? Is someone missing from the picture that would add to the feeling of success? What kind of sacrifice did it require for your character to get what they wanted?

Brandy Miller

My Talents

Your character's talents are those things that come naturally to him or her. They take no effort on their part to learn, and they will advance more quickly in ability than students without talent when they do apply themselves and actively work to improve. Some talents may remain hidden and unseen until the character is put in a position where they come to the surface. Other talents are things the character has been doing almost all of their lives.

What subjects in school come naturally to me?

Answering this question from your character's perspective can help you begin to identify their talents, since school is one of the first areas that children begin actively learning things. If your character picked up a foreign language quickly and almost effortlessly, it can signal a hidden talent for linguistics. If he or she was good in English or reading, it can signal a talent for writing. If geometry was something that came naturally to your character, it can signal a talent for spatial relationships, for figuring out how objects interact in space.

What are people always asking me to do for them?

Since our talents come so effortlessly to us, we may think nothing of them. However, other people will notice them and ask us to use them on their behalf. What are things that other people have always asked your character for help doing? What do other people say about your character when introducing them to other people? For example, "You should meet Barry. He's a whiz at math!"

What is easy for me to do, but hard for other people to do?

Whether it's drawing, writing, speaking in front of people, singing, solving math problems, or creating things, our talents make it easy for us to do things that other people would find daunting or even impossible. What are some things that your character has always found easy to do but that everyone else says is hard?

What do I do well without much effort?

While even the most naturally gifted musician has to put some effort into learning an instrument, the truly talented can learn in days what it takes some people months or even years to grasp. Thinking about your character, what can he or she do well without real effort? What things has he or she learned much more quickly than the people around him or her?

What do I enjoy doing?

We usually enjoy doing things that we are good at doing. These things don't feel like work to us because they come so easily and bring so much enjoyment. These activities usually fall into areas that reflect our talents. Thinking about your character, what are activities that he or she really enjoys doing? Does he or she like to sing in the shower? Does he or she keep a hidden journal?

Exercise:

Step 1: Choose some talents for your character that will be useful to helping them solve their main problem and write these on your character sheet. These do not have to be talents they know that they have. They may be hidden talents, waiting to be uncovered or fully realized. If they are hidden write an H in parenthesis (H) beside them.

Step 2: Write a story in which your character either uses one of his or her talents to help someone else or discovers a talent he or she didn't realize s/he had. How does this change your character's perspective about their talent or about themselves?

Creating A Character Backstory

My Skills

In addition to talents, your character has developed some skills throughout their life. These skills may have come through school, through self-teaching, through a mentor or other trainer, or through on-the-job experience. These are the skills your character can use whenever they get themselves into a tight corner or when they need to do something to help someone else. Skills can be classified into seven essential categories: survival, street, professional, academic, political, and spiritual.

Survival skills

Survival skills are any skills your character has that would allow him or her to survive in a wilderness environment. Does your character know how to hunt? Can he or she fish? Have they ever been taught how to garden? Do they know how to navigate terrain using a compass and a map? Can they track someone or something across the terrain? Do they know how to tell animal tracks apart from one another? Do they know how to build a rough shelter if they should get caught out in the open? Do they know how to tell which plants are edible and which aren't? Do they know which plants have medicinal qualities and how to use those?

Street skills

Street skills are any skills your character has that would allow him or her to survive on the streets in an urban or suburban environment. Does your character know where to find shelter in their city in case they find themselves homeless? Do they know what the local gangs are and how to identify them? Can they navigate the subway or public transportation system? Do they know how to spot a drug buy? Can they identify someone who is using drugs? Do they know where to buy alcohol if they are underage? Can they drive a car?

Professional Skills

Professional skills are directly related to a trade or profession that your character might know. Doctors, lawyers, teachers, policemen, firemen, graphic artists, and computer programmers all have a range of skills tied to their specific profession that help them to do their job in daily life. However, those same skills can be transferred to other environments and can help them overcome the problems they face. Other professions are carpenters, masons, electricians, plumbers, vehicle repair technicians, and computer repair technicians.

Academic Skills

Academic skills would include all those things that help your character to succeed in learning or teaching something to someone. They include skills like reading, researching, writing, interviewing, and test taking. These skills can come in handy when your character needs to learn something new or when your character needs to find information either online or in a library.

Political Skills

These skills do not just apply to those who bear the title of politician. Politics is all about being able to get people to work with and for you on a project, handling egos diplomatically, and motivating people to work toward a common objective. Political skills can be applied to any group of people, because where there are people, there are politics. Does your character know how to debate? Do they know how to skillfully negotiate terms? Do they know how to encourage someone to change their minds? These would all be examples of political skills.

Spiritual Skills

Spiritual skills are not just for priests, bishops, or deacons. Lay people can have them as well. These are the skills that inspire people to become their best selves, can make present the supernatural world for others, and can motivate people to act for motives other than their own self-interest. These skills include prayer, prophecy, speaking in tongues, discernment, spiritual healing, and exhortation.

Exercise:

Step 1. Choose some skills for your character that will be useful in helping them to overcome his or her main problem. Write these on your character sheet.

Step 2. Write a short story showing how your character developed one of his or her skills. Who taught them or where did they learn it? How long did it take them to develop this skill? Did they expect to ever use this skill again?

Creating A Character Backstory

The Best (and Worst) About Me

Like every human being, your character has strengths and weaknesses. These personality flaws add to the depth of the character and allow the reader to identify more strongly with them. If your character were always perfect, they might be someone that readers wished to be more like but would also be someone readers would likely see as unattainable and unrealistic. The vices which most people succumb to are pride, anger, envy, greed, laziness, ambition, cowardice, and lust. The virtues, or strengths, which most people display to one degree or another are mercy, gratitude, discipline, love, humility, faith, hope, and courage.

Faith versus ambition

Ambition is the tendency that all human beings have to want to control other people and the world around them. A strong faith in something greater than themselves can help your character combat this temptation because they will recognize that such control is an impossibility for them and is not their job anyway. They will be able to let go of power and delegate better, recognizing those who have skills in areas where they are weak.

Hope versus greed

Greed is the tendency of the human heart to settle for short-term pleasures rather than pursuing long-term gains.

Hope is that inner voice that whispers to us that there are better things than this out there for us if we are willing to do the work to make them happen. Hope can help your character stay motivated to keep trying for better things, even when the only examples that surround them are of failure and broken dreams.

Love versus lust

Lust is the human tendency to pursue sexual pleasure rather than genuine intimacy with other people. This is not to say that sexual pleasure cannot be had along with intimacy, but that the lustful person pursues pleasure as a substitute for intimacy rather than seeing it as being part of genuine intimacy. Love is the choice to pursue the greater good of the other person over your own personal pleasure, and so it helps your character to fight their inner tendency toward lust.

Humility versus pride

Pride is that tendency of the human person to see themselves as greater than, or better than, other people. It leads them to treat people disrespectfully or condescendingly, prevents them from seeing what others have to offer, and leads to stunted emotional growth as a result. Humility is the ability to recognize what is good about yourself without losing sight of the value of those around you. Humility can help your character defeat their pride and grow emotionally.

Gratitude versus envy

Envy is the tendency of the human heart to believe that what someone else has is better than what we have. It leads people to steal, cheat, and lie in order to get what they believe the other person has. Gratitude allows us to see the good things in our own life and our own circumstances and to be happy for those things so that we no longer desire the things that other people have. It also helps us to see the particular burdens that come with the things other people have, and to appreciate what we have all the more because of it. Gratitude can help your character become a more cheerful and contented person.

Discipline versus laziness

Laziness is the human tendency to avoid doing what we know we should be doing to help others or ourselves. Discipline is that internal mechanism that motivates us to move past our laziness and take action even when we don't feel like it. Like a spiritual muscle, discipline is strengthened each time we make the right choice.

Courage versus cowardice

Cowardice is the human tendency to avoid personal sacrifice when we know that making such a sacrifice is the only way to help others. Courage is the decision to put the lives of others ahead of our own, even when we know it will require sacrificing something we value – including our own lives.

Mercy versus anger

Anger is the human tendency to hold on to the pain others cause us and to allow this feeling to drive us to action against the person who hurt us. Mercy is the decision made to treat others as we want to be treated rather than as we have been treated and to offer forgiveness for the failings that drove that person to hurt us.

Exercise

Step 1. On your character sheet, fill in the dots to indicate how weak or strong your character is in each of these areas.

Step 2. Write a short story in which your character confronts one of his or her weaknesses. Do they succumb to the weakness or overcome it? How do they feel about how the situation is resolved?

| Creating A Character Backstory

The Secrets I Keep

Everyone has secrets. Some of these secrets we keep about ourselves, some we keep about others. These secrets form a protective wall that protect us and those we love, but those walls are also barriers that make it harder for other people to get to know us. This is just as true about your character as it is about anyone else in life. The struggle to keep a secret, to reveal a secret, or to find out the truth about a secret can provide excellent fodder for the story you want to write.

What is my greatest secret?

What is the secret that your character hasn't shared with anyone else, or possibly with only one other person? Keeping this secret from others will determine how they handle other people's efforts to get to know them better. For example, if your character's greatest secret is that they murdered someone, they will do everything they can to stop other people from finding out about the murder. On a less dramatic note, but no less significant, if the character's biggest secret is that they aren't worth loving, they will push away any effort on the part of other people to get to know them better for fear they'll discover that secret. It doesn't matter that their "secret" may have no basis in reality. A character can believe themselves guilty of murder but be innocent of the crime. In fact, many of the secrets people keep aren't grounded in reality but in fear cloaking itself as reality. The important thing is that your character BELIEVES it is true. How will your character react if his or her secret is discovered? How will he or she treat the person who reveals that secret to others?

What secrets do I keep about my family?

Every family has its share of secrets. The drug or alcohol addicted parent, the pedophile grandparent, the cross dressing cousin, the crazy aunt, the uncle who joined a cult are all examples of secrets that families might be keeping. These secrets will shape how the character behaves around certain family members, how eager they are to have other people get to know their family, and what steps they may be willing to take to protect their family's secret. It doesn't even matter if nobody else in the world would actually care about the secrets this character is keeping, what matters is how damaging your character and his or her family believes those secrets to be. What happens if your character accidentally lets that secret out? How will the family treat your character? How will your character react if someone else lets that secret out?

What secrets do I keep about my best friend?

Best friends know practically everything about one another, and usually their fair share of secrets. What secrets is your character keeping for his or her best friend? How does that secret keep the two of them tied together? How far is your character willing to go to protect his or her best friend's secret? What steps have they already taken? What would happen to the friendship if this secret got out?

Creating A Character Backstory

What secrets do I keep about my lover?

A spouse or intimate partner is often the one person who knows even those secrets you haven't told your best friend. Living with your character day in and day out means they've seen sides of your character no one else has, and have a better chance to put together the pieces of the puzzle. This is why people who harbor the nastiest secrets often have no truly close relationships. There is too high a risk of discovery. What secrets does your character keep about his or her lover? How does this secret shape their relationship? What steps has your character taken to protect his partner from discovery? How far is he or she willing to go to protect this secret? What would happen if the secret got out?

What other secrets am I keeping?

What other pieces of information does your character know that would damage someone if the truth were revealed? Does he work for the military or the government? Does he work for a bank or other financial institution? Does he know something about his boss or his co-workers?

Exercise

Step 1. Choose up to five secrets that your character is keeping. At least one of these secrets should relate to the story. Write them on the character sheet.

Step 2. Write a short story in which your character encounters one of the secrets he or she is keeping. How does your character feel about the secret initially? Does he or she feel the same way now? Does your character realize the consequences of talking about this secret?

| Creating A Character Backstory

What Don't I Know?

Just as your character keeps secrets from other people, other people are keeping secrets from your character. These secrets can drive plot as your character works to find out the truth about these secrets, or can be life-altering events when your character discovers these secrets and then struggles to make meaning of them.

What does my family know about me that I don't know?

Was your character adopted? Is your character's family a member of a secret organization? Does your character's family have ties to an illegal organization? Has your character's family been lying to your character about how much money they have or where they come from? What would it change about your character's life if he or she found out the truth? How long has this secret been kept? How far has the family gone to keep the secret from your character? Why have they kept this a secret?

What does my best friend know about me that I don't?

Has your character's best friend overheard something and kept it from your character? Have they witnessed something and don't want your character to find out? Have they done something to hurt your character that they are hiding? Why have they been keeping this a secret? How long have they kept it secret? What do they fear would happen if your character found out? How far have they gone to keep this a secret?

What does my enemy know about me that I don't?

Has your character's enemy done something to your character that your character hasn't found out about yet? Has your character's enemy seen or heard something that would be damaging to your character if it were known? Has the enemy met someone from your character's past? Is the enemy aware of someone who is planning something against your character? Why isn't your enemy using this information against your character yet? How long have they known? What do they plan to do with the information?

What does my lover know about me that I don't?

Has your character's lover found information about your past and kept it from your character? Have they seen or overheard something, positive or negative, and kept it from your character? Have they done something behind your character's back to hurt or help them? Are they planning to do something with or to your character but haven't revealed it yet? Why are they keeping this a secret? What do they plan to do with the information? How far are they willing to go to keep it a secret? What are their plans if your character finds out?

Who else knows something about me that I don't?

Is there a stranger, government official, teacher, co-worker, boss, or classmate that knows something about your character that your character doesn't know? How did they obtain the information? How long have they had it? What are they planning to do with it? What would happen to your

Creating A Character Backstory

character if that information were found out? How would your character's life change if other people knew this information?

Exercise

Step 1. Choose up to five secrets that are being kept about your character by other people. Write these down on the character sheet. Note who is keeping the secret beside each one.

Step 2. Write a short story in which your character discovers that someone else knows his secret. How does the discovery happen? Does your character know who knows it? Who does your character suspect might know it? How does your character feel about the discovery? What is your character planning to do about this discovery?

Brandy Miller

The Worst Day of My Life

Your character's life is full of moments and memories. What day in their life stands out in their memory as the worst day? This is a day that changed them profoundly, shaping and forming their future choices. It is possible for this day to happen just before the story you write begins, and may even be the cause of the action that takes place during your story.

What happened?

What was it about this day that made it so terrible? Did they lose something valuable to them? Did someone your character cared about get hurt, nearly die, or even die? Did your character get hurt, nearly die, or actually die? Did someone discover something embarrassing or damaging about their past?

Who was involved?

Was your character alone the day of this event? Did they know everyone present or were strangers involved? Did someone your character know make the day worse than it already was? Who wasn't there that your character thinks would have made it better? How did this change the relationship between your character and the people involved for better or for worse?

Who knows about the event?

Aside from the people that were directly involved, who else knows about the event? Has this changed how they treat your character? Is this something they discuss with your character or is it too uncomfortable to bring up while your character is in the room?

How do I feel when I think about this day?

How does your character feel when he or she thinks about this day? Does your character ever talk about this event with others? How does your character react when this event is brought up in their presence? Why do they feel this way?

How did this day change me?

Does your character feel that their life has changed for the better or for the worse because of this event? What lessons did they learn about life from this event? How does the memory of this event help them achieve their hopes or add to their fears? What did your character realize about him or herself as a result of this event?

What would I do differently if I could?

What does your character think was the cause of the events that day? Do they feel they could have done something to stop it from happening? Does your character blame himself for it or does he blame someone else?

Exercise

Write a short story about this day answer each of the questions outlined in this chapter.

Creating A Character Backstory

The Best Day of My Life

Just as the worst day affects your character's decisions and helps to shape who they are, so does the best day of their life. Memories of the best day can inspire them to keep going when they are tempted to quit, cheer them up when they are unhappy, or even lead them to try and make other people feel the same way they did that day.

What happened to make this the best day?

Did they meet their best friend or lover? Did they accomplish some goal or achieve something they didn't think they could? Were they recognized for something they did well? Did they overcome a fear or defeat an obstacle? Did they receive praise from an unlikely source or from someone whose opinion they valued highly?

Who was involved?

Were they alone on this day? Were they surrounded with friends and family? Was it a part of a special celebration or did it happen on an ordinary day? Were there strangers present? How many people were there?

Who knows about the event?

How many people know about this event? Is it a private thing, where only family and friends know, or was it a larger event that impacted several people in the community? Was it publicized in any way?

How do I feel when I think about this day?

When your character thinks back on this day, how does he or she feel? Does he or she like to talk about the event? How long ago did the event take place? Is this memory tinged with sadness or any other negative emotion because of something that happened afterward?

How did this day change me?

What lessons did your character learn about life because of this event? What aspects of his or her character were revealed during this day? Did it change the relationships he had with friends, family, or other individuals? Did he or she begin to have hope for the first time that their greatest dream might be possible? Did your character change their goals or overcome their fears through this day?

What could have made it better?

Was there someone missing from that day your character wishes had been there? A parent? Teacher? Friend? Did something happen that nearly threatened to make things go wrong? Did the character not fully appreciate how great this day was because of something else going on in his or her life at the time?

Exercise

Write a short story about this day answer each of the questions outlined in this chapter.

Creating A Character Backstory

My First Love and My Current Love Interest

Your first love

The first love your character has will forever imprint themselves on his or her heart. Every future romantic encounter will be held up to the first to see how it compares. Thus, knowing the first love of your character is an important part of portraying them realistically.

Who are you?

What is the name of your character's first love? What did he or she look like? How did they dress? How did they act towards other people? What did their voice sound like?

How did we meet?

Where and when did your character meet their first love? How old were they when they met? Was it love at first sight or did it take a while for one of the lovers to grow on the other?

Are we still together?

How long did the romance last? If they are still together, how long have they been together? What keeps the relationship going? What problems have they overcome together?

Why did we break up?

If your character is not still with his or her first love, what caused the break up? Was it a choice on the part of your character or were they dumped? Did death come between them? Did someone move? Does either your character or the love interest secretly harbor a desire to get back together? What would prohibit this from happening?

How long ago did we break up?

How long has it been since your character and his or her first love were together? How does your character feel about the break up now? How did he or she feel then?

Are you still a part of my life?

Although they may not be lovers anymore, is there something that keeps the two of them connected? Do they have a child together? Do they work at the same company? Do they own a business together? How is their relationship? Are they able to be friends or is one partner unable to let go of the past and move on? How do they feel about having their first love still in their life?

Your current love

If your character is not still together with his or her first love, do they have a current partner? This person will have a tremendous influence on the decisions that your character makes and on their view of the world. When things are going well with their current love, the world will seem brighter, more cheery, and everything will seem possible. When things aren't going well with their current love, the world can seem dark and grim no matter how brightly the sun may actually be shining. Furthermore, your character will often do things they wouldn't ordinarily be willing to do simply to please their current partner.

Who is my current love?

What is the name of your character's current love? What does he or she look like? How do they dress? How do they act towards other people? What interests or hobbies do they have? Where do they work or go to school? What does their voice sound like? What do they smell like?

How did we meet?

Where and when did your character meet their current partner? How old were they when they met? Was it love at first sight or did it take a while for one of the lovers to grow on the other? What attracted your character to this person at first?

How does my current love feel about my first love?

Does your character have a current love interest? Does your character's first love know your character's current love interest? How do the two of them feel about each other? Does your character's current love interest feel any jealousy toward your character's first love? How are they different? In what ways are they the same?

Exercise

Brandy Miller

Step 1. Fill in the area entitled "My First Love" and "My Current Love" on your character sheet.

Step 2. Write a short story in which either your character or your character's current love interest encounters your character's first love. How does he or she feel about the encounter? Do they recognize this person at first? Does this person recognize him or her? How does he or she react to the encounter? How have the two characters changed since their last meeting?

Creating A Character Backstory

My Best Friend

Your character, at some point in his or her life, has had a best friend. That person may or may not be in their life right now, but they will always have a special place in the life of your character. If they are currently in your character's life, they may act as the sidekick or even the herald. After all, best friends know you well enough that they aren't afraid to call you on it when they see you doing something stupid and they love you enough to help you do whatever it takes to overcome the problems you're facing.

Who are you?

Who is your character's best friend? What is his name? What is his age? What does he look like? What are his hobbies and talents? What are his skills? How much does your character know about his or her life?

How did we meet?

The details of how the character and his best friend met can set the tone for the kind of relationship they form. If they met at a bar over a couple of beers, for instance, the relationship isn't likely to be the same as someone who met their best friend during combat. Two drinkers who bond over alcohol can feel close and share a lot in common – but what happens when one of them goes to AA and stops drinking? Two single ladies who are both looking for love and dreaming of family may have a lot in common and get along really well, but what happens a few years later when one is married and has her first kid and the other one is still single?

What makes you special?

What is it about the best friend that made them best friends? Could they share anything with them? Were they the most exciting person to be around? Did they throw the best parties? Did they help your character overcome a fear or failing? Your character undoubtedly gained something just by being around that person, whether the something was fame, fortune, or confidence. Whatever it is that made that person special to your character, find it and use it.

Are we still best friends?

Is your character still best friends with his best friend? If not, what happened? How long ago did they break up? If so, how has that best friend made your character's life better? Has the relationship grown deeper, stayed the same, or started to drift? The problem your character faces may well be a catalyst to bring the two best friends back together if they've stopped being friends, or to stop the drift and bring them closer, or it may end up being something that drives a wedge between the two of them.

How do I feel about you?

How does your character feel about his best friend? If the relationship broke up, your character may be harboring a grudge against his former best friend. He may not want to forgive them, or may not think he can. Part of his conflict may

Creating A Character Backstory

be that he must forgive his best friend and get his help in order to solve the problem. He may want to reconcile, but the best friend is the one holding the grudge. He may not know where the former best friend lives and may want to find him.

Exercise

Step 1. Fill in the area entitled "My Best Friend" on your character sheet.

Step 2. Write a short story in which your character encounters his or her best friend. How does your character feel about the encounter? Do they recognize this person at first? Does this person recognize your character? How does he or she react to the encounter? How have the two characters changed since their last meeting?

Brandy Miller

My Worst Enemy

Just as our family and friends shape us, so do our enemies. Your character's worst enemy has had a big impact on their life. After all, it takes a lot of pain before we add someone to a list of people we never want to see again and may even wish were dead. Examining who this person is and the history your character has with them can not only inspire you, but help you grow in your understanding of the character and his behavior.

Who are you?

What is the name, age, and appearance of your character's worst enemy? What does he or she sound like when she or he speaks? How does he walk? What is his style? What does he like to eat?

How did we meet?

How did your character meet his worst enemy? Did they go to school together? Do they work together? Are they family members? Where they met tells you something about your character, and something about the nature of their relationship.

What did you do to me?

What did your character's worst enemy do to earn such a status? Were they the school bully who picked on your character relentlessly? Are they a boss that stole all their best ideas and took the credit? To earn the status of worst enemy, the actions taken must have been pretty awful.

Why do you hate me?

Why does your character's worst enemy hate them so much? Most people don't hate without some kind of motivation, whether it's envy, or a misunderstanding, or a slight that went unaddressed. It's even possible that your character's worst enemy doesn't hate them at all – they may not care about them or even think about them as a person.

How do I loathe thee? Let me count the ways!

How much venom is there in your character's hatred of his or her worst enemy? How far would they be willing to go to get revenge? Is this a slow, simmering hatred or a hot, burning fire of hate? Why can't they forgive this person?

One thing to remember when creating a worst enemy is that every time your character encounters someone who reminds them of this person, they are likely to turn this loathing on that person – even if they don't deserve it. This can make for some very interesting personal dynamics between characters in your story.

Exercise

Step 1. Fill in the area entitled "My Worst Enemy" on your character sheet.

Step 2. Write a short story in which your character encounters his or her worst enemy. How does your character feel about the encounter? Do they recognize this person at first? Does this person recognize your character? How does he or she react to the encounter? How have the two characters changed since their last meeting?

Creating A Character Backstory

Meet My Family

Family shapes us

The people that raise us have a huge role to play in shaping who we are and who we become. Your character's family will have the same influence on him or her. Knowing who the family is, what they are like, and how the character views his family goes a long way towards helping you to write a character that is believable and authentic. Furthermore, the family can often be a source of inspiration and help for the character in time of trouble.

Who is my mother?

The first person in anyone's life is their mother. Even before meeting the outside world and its inhabitants, her voice is heard, her heartbeat is felt, it is the foods and drinks that she takes in that are tasted and absorbed, and the body moves to the rhythms of the mother's movements. The intimacy of this connection has a lifelong influence on the development of a person, and your character will be no different. Even if the birth mother gave the character up for adoption, there will be a part of them that knows something is missing in their life. Once the child is born, how they are treated by their mother will largely define for them how they view women, how they expect to be treated by women, and what they believe it means to be a woman.

Who is my father?

A character's view of men and what it means to be a man is shaped by his father, even when the father isn't present. So even if your character is the child of a deadbeat dad, or a father who died when the child was young, it's still important to sketch some details about the father. Is the father still a presence in the life of the mother? What is the relationship between the father and the mother of your character? If he's gone, why did he leave? Does your character know the reason or does he think it's because of something else?

My siblings

Siblings also have a role to play in shaping who we become. Does your character have a lot of siblings, so that family gatherings are huge, noisy affairs or does he just have one or two so that family gatherings are small and quiet? What is his relationship to each of his siblings? Does he have one sibling that he is particularly close to? Does he have a sibling who hates him or that he actively hates? Why?

My grandparents

Grandparents can have a special place in the life of a character, just as they do in our own. What kind of grandparents were they? Were they distant, rarely visiting? Did they live with your character for a time? Were they harsh and cold or warm and nurturing? What did your character learn from his grandparents? Are the grandparents still living? What kind of relationship does he have with each of his grandparents?

Aunts, uncles, cousins

Creating A Character Backstory

How well does your character know his aunts, uncles, and cousins? What kind of relationship do they have? How often do they visit? Where do they live?

Creating a family for your character can seem like a lot of work, but in answering these questions you will learn more about your character, give yourself people and situations from their past that they can use to help solve problems, and make them more believable to the reader.

Exercise:

Step 1. Fill out the pedigree chart for your character's parents, grandparents, and great-grandparents

Step 2. Fill in a family group sheet for each father/mother pairing on the family group sheet.

Step 3. Write a short story in which your character attends a family reunion. Who is present at the family reunion? Who are they glad to see? Who is there that your character wishes weren't? Who is not there that your character wishes were?

Brandy Miller

My Mother, My Father, and I

Relationships and memories

Relationships are built on memories. In order to create a believable relationship, you need to create memories for your character of the time spent with his mother and his father. If that parent is not present in the life of the character, these memories may be of their absence, or of the favorite things they did to fill in that gap in their life – such as imagining what they would do if his father or mother were there. These memories all come with feelings, and can inspire your character to act in unexpected ways when confronted with them. Whenever your character sees similar events played out, these emotions will return along with the memories of his own past.

Earliest memory

Creating a foundation for later events, the earliest memory a character has sets the tone for the relationship that evolves. Is it a happy memory? A sad memory? When your character looks at that memory in his mind, what are the feelings that come to mind? Remorse? Bitterness? Longing? Whatever feelings he or she has, exploring why those feelings exist can lead to insights about what happened next.

Favorite time together

What was the favorite activity that your character engaged in with his or her mother? Was it gardening? Shopping? Going to the movies? The bedtime story? Cooking together? Dancing? How did they feel when those activities were going on? Do they still do these things together? When did it stop, if it has? What caused it to stop?

The worst memory

What is the worst memory your character carries of his mother or father? Did his father or mother do something to him? Did he discover something about him or her that disappointed him? Did he or she do something that disappointed the character? Did they fight? Has he forgiven his parent for whatever happened, if it was the parent's fault, or himself for doing it, if it was his own? What has he done to try and fix whatever happened that day? How did it change their relationship?

How I saw my parent as a child

How did your character view his parent as a child? Did he want to be like that parent? Did he find that parent intimidating? Was he frightened of his mother or his father? What would the character never dream of doing as a child for fear his father or mother would find out?

How I saw my parent as a teenager

Children's view of their parents often changes during the teenage years as they discover more about the parents' strengths and weaknesses. Did his view of his parent change for the better or the worse? What weaknesses did he discover about his parent that caused the view to change for the worse? What strengths did he discover his parent had that caused the view to change for the better? Did he want to be like his parent? Was he embarrassed by his parent?

How I see my parent now

How does your character see his parent now? Are they close? Does they talk often? Does he admire his parent? Does he pity his parent? Has he stopped talking to his parent? What could his parent do to change that situation? Has the parent tried to reconcile? What efforts has the parent made? Why weren't they successful?

Exercise

Choose either your character's father or your character's mother. Write a short story detailing an event from your character's past involving this parent. How does your character feel about the event? Why makes this particular moment in their life stand out? How does this moment influence your character's current life?

Creating A Character Backstory

Life at Home

What was life like for your character when he was living at home? What is life like if he's still at home? What is it going to be like should he stop by to visit? Answering these questions creates a richer portrait of your character, but can help you to gain inspiration when you need it.

My parents together

Were the parents of your character married? Divorced? Separated? Never married? Is your father still in your mother's life? How do they behave when they are together now? How did they behave when they were together? How has the relationship between the parents of your character formed and shaped the way he sees long term relationships? Sex? Children? Marriage?

Sibling rivalries

Do sibling rivalries exist in your character's family? In your character's life, who is the preferred sibling? What sibling role does your character tend to play? Responsible elder, black sheep, baby of the family, peace maker? Which sibling does your character's mother prefer? Which sibling does your character's father prefer? How has this hurt your character? Is your character trying to change his role?

Family time

Does your character's family spend time together? When your character's family does get together to do things, where are they likely to go? What are they likely to do? Do they take vacations together? Do they go hiking or camping together?

Holidays and traditions

What holidays does your character's family celebrate? What holidays does your character's family ignore? Is there a reason? What traditions does your family have for the holidays? For birthdays? For other celebrations? What does your character like or dislike about those holidays and traditions?

Faith and morals

What is the faith tradition your character's family follows? Whose faith is strongest in the family? Does your character's mother and father share a faith, or do they follow different faiths? Has this created conflict in the family? How does your character's family define good and bad, right and wrong? What is the one thing that everyone knows not to do? What action could a family member take to get them disowned by the parents?

Neighbors and Your Neighborhood

No home would be complete without the neighbors that make up your neighborhood. Funny or strange, warm and welcoming or distant and antagonistic, it is the neighbors in your neighborhood that are part and parcel of the memories

Creating A Character Backstory

you have about going home. Who lives next door to your family's home? Are they the same people you grew up with or have those people moved? Are people in your neighborhood fairly stable or are they mostly transient? Do the neighbors know each other well or do they keep to themselves? Are there any particularly unpleasant or strange neighbors that live nearby?

Exercise:

Your character has just walked through the door of his or her parent's house. Write a short story about what your character encounters while he or she is there. Is this house the same house he or she grew up in or is it the same? What is different about home from when he or she was growing up? What has remained the same? How does your character feel as he or she walks through the door? Who greets him or her? Who avoids him or her? What memories are called up as he or she interacts with the objects in the environment?

Notes

Creating A Character Backstory

Brandy Miller

Creating A Character Backstory

Brandy Miller

Creating A Character Backstory

Brandy Miller

Creating A Character Backstory

Brandy Miller

Creating A Character Backstory

Brandy Miller

Creating A Character Backstory

Brandy Miller

Creating A Character Backstory

Brandy Miller

Creating A Character Backstory

Brandy Miller

Creating A Character Backstory

Brandy Miller

Creating A Character Backstory

Brandy Miller

Creating A Character Backstory

Brandy Miller

Creating A Character Backstory

Brandy Miller

Printed in Great Britain
by Amazon

Creating A Character Backstory